# MERRY FISHMAS

Original title: Βυθούγεννα, the Fishsoup book series
International Title: Merry Fishmas
Author: George Lebesis
Illustrator: Tamsin Baker
Translator: Jeannette A. Arduino
Text editor: James Wootton
Proofreading: Barbara Botell

ISBN: 979-8-89496-242-9

Copyright @ 2024 by Webra Group Ltd.
Webra Group Ltd
Pinewood Studios
Iver Heath SL0 0NH UK
www.webragroup.com
info@webragroup.com

All rights reserved. In accordance with the The UK Copyright, Designs and Patents Act 1988, the scanning, uploading, and electronic sharing of any part of this book without the permission of the publisher is unlawful piracy and theft of the author's intellectual property. If you would like to use material of the book (other than for review purposes), prior written permission must be obtained by contacting the publisher at info@webragroup.com. The publisher is not responsible for websites (or their content) that are not owned by the publisher.

It doesn't feel like December on the legendary island of Milos, as the sun continues to shine brightly and the clear blue sky stubbornly keeps winter at bay. And to think, in just a few days, it will be Christmas!

In the famous taverna, *The Steamed Oyster,* all is quiet, as it's still very early in the morning. In fact, it's so early that the chefs haven't yet started preparing for the day.

The only one who seems restless is King Adonis, a colourful and chubby tropical fish with puffed-out little cheeks, swimming around and around in the taverna's aquarium. Mr Costas, the owner of the taverna, brought him back from faraway China. He's so different from all the other fish that swim in the waters of Milos that people from every corner of the island come to *The Steamed Oyster* to enjoy a bowl of fish soup and admire him.

Anastasia, Mr Costas's daughter, is watching her favourite cartoon on the television when suddenly a news flash disrupts the taverna's tranquillity:

"My dear fellow citizens," begins Mr Funless, the Minister of Holidays and Entertainment. "I have had to make a sad decision due to the hard times we are living in: This year, **there will be no Christmas.**"

Anastasia gasps in horror and slaps both hands over her open mouth.

"All holidays are banned," continues Mr Funless. "We will not decorate, eat roast turkey or Christmas pudding, and above all, we will not exchange gifts. Schools will remain open, and we will all pretend it's not Christmas. This way, we will not spend any money, and in the future, we will be better off."

The minister's words leave everyone shocked. A few people are pleased they won't have to waste money this year, but most are saddened because they need the joy that Christmas brings. Even Mr Costas is disappointed with the news—and we know how stingy he is!

"What!" shouts Anastasia. "How can we not have Christmas?" She throws one of her slippers at the television.

"Calm down, my little Anastasia," says Pierre, the French chef, in his French accent. "It's not so serious! You will see how easy it is to live without holidays." But Anastasia grows angrier and angrier.

"It's not just any holiday; it's **Christmas!**" replies Anastasia, storming off to call her friend.

"Yanni!" she barks at the screen. "Come quickly to the taverna... No, I can't wait. Come now! And don't be late."

Meanwhile, all is calm at the bottom of Bubble Buddies Bay. Apollo the Goby searches the sand for morsels of food while he waits for Dimitra the Octopus, who is stirring a pot of bubbling seaweed heated by electric eels. Athena the Flying Fish sings, practising her scales (musical scales, not fish scales). Theo the Urchin bounces around from rock to rock, while Carci the Crab shows Vassili the Clownfish how she picks up a rock with her claw and throws it.

It's a typical day like any other. Nothing exciting has happened for some time now, so our Bubble Buddies have become somewhat bored.

Meanwhile, back on dry land, Yanni arrives at *The Steamed Oyster* quicker than a migrating Swallowfish. He taps on the aquarium glass while chirping, "Morning, Adonis!" King Adonis swims up to the glass with a big smile.

Yanni sits down with Anastasia at one of the taverna's dining tables. "What's so urgent, Anastasia?" he asks. "I missed my breakfast." Anastasia isn't smiling. "Have a bread roll—haven't you heard?"
"Heard what?" says Yanni, biting into a bread roll.
## "They're cancelling Christmas!"
Yanni nearly chokes on his bread roll, then looks at Anastasia, wide-eyed in disbelief.

"Time for school!" Mr Costas calls out from the kitchen.

"How can we go to school when they're going to cancel Christmas?" Anastasia shouts to her father.

"Calm down now. Remember, money is life; it's all about the money," Mr Costas says with a smile.

Anastasia doesn't agree. "But, Daddy, it's Christmas! You know, about sharing and caring and friendship and a thousand other good things that don't cost money."

"Children, just calm down and go to school," says Mr Costas, not wanting to hear any more.

"But, Mr Costas," says Yanni, "nobody will come to the taverna for Christmas dinner." Mr Costas just laughs. "People will always come to The Steamed Oyster, my boy, to see King Adonis. He brings in the people, whether it's Christmas or not."

Anastasia is furious, and then she has an idea.

Theo the Urchin decides to take a trip to the surface to his favourite rock and enjoy a little sunbathing. Just as he settles down, something catches his eye; two children are running towards the shore. It's Anastasia and Yanni.

"Run, Yanni! Let's set King Adonis free before they notice anything," shouts Anastasia.

"What a fantastic idea, Anastasia. Now your dad will see how important Christmas is. Without Adonis, nobody will set foot in the taverna."

Anastasia and Yanni are ready to set King Adonis free in the bay, happy to teach the chefs in the taverna a lesson.

"One—two—and three!" Anastasia and Yanni shout and throw King Adonis into the sea. **"Have a good trip, Adonis!"**

Without missing a beat, Theo dives into the water and follows King Adonis as he swims down to the seabed.

"I'm free! At last, I'm free!" cries King Adonis excitedly.

"Hello, colourful fish. What's your name?" asks Theo.

"My name is King Adonis, I'm a tropical fish from China!"

"From China?" Theo exclaims in surprise. "And what are you doing here in the Mediterranean Sea?"

"I was living in the aquarium of the taverna, but now I'm free! The children set me free. Oh, the poor children."

"What happened to the children?"

The Bubble Buddies gather around Theo and King Adonis, all wondering about the strange and very peculiar fish on their seabed.

King Adonis begins to tell them all about the taverna and how the children helped him escape the aquarium when, "Oh, but the poor children," sighs King Adonis. **"They've banned their Christmas."**

"Oh no!" cries Apollo, then he whispers to Athena, "What's Christmas?"

"Are these children called Anastasia and Yanni?" asks Athena.

"Yes! Do you know them?"

"It's the same darling children who helped me escape the taverna's aquarium." Athena looks at all the other Bubble Buddies. "And remember when Mr Costas tried to make fish soup out of us all?"

"We can't leave the children without Christmas," says Athena. "We have to do something about it." Everybody agrees.

"Good," pipes up Theo. "But does anyone know what Christmas is?"

They all look at each other. Theo is right. Nobody knows what Christmas is.

Mr Costas looks through the glass of the aquarium.
"Where's King Adonis? **Adonis!** Pierre! Pierre!"
Pierre sticks his head around the kitchen door.
"Yes, Mr Costas?"
"Have you seen King Adonis?"
"Is he not in the aquarium?"
Mr Costas puts his hands on his head and flattens his chef's hat in frustration. Without King Adonis or Christmas dinner, he will be ruined.
"Pierre!"
"Yes, Mr Costas?"
"We are left with no choice."

There is only one way to know what Christmas is, and that is to visit the wise Anglerfish, Atlas. Without another thought, the Bubble Buddies make their way down to Atlas's cave.

It takes a while to get there, but when they arrive, Theo wastes no time and rings the bell near the entrance, calling out: "Mr Atlas! Mr Atlas! Could you please come out?"

As soon as Atlas appears outside his dark cave, Theo speaks.
"We don't want to bother you, but we have something important to ask," begins Theo.
"No problem at all, go ahead," says Atlas cheerfully, "besides, I'm used to you by now."
Theo explains the story told by their new friend King Adonis and then asks, "So, what is Christmas?"

Atlas slowly approaches them, opens his big fins, and in one move, embraces them, saying tenderly: "This is Christmas."
"Christmas is a hug?" wonders Dimitra, rather pleased but somewhat squeezed.
"Folks believe that two thousand years ago," begins Atlas, "the people were more than ever in need of a warm embrace. It was then that Jesus Christ was born and he showed them the way. He spoke to them about love and how special it is to make the person next to you happy, how wonderful it is to share and care for others, and to love yourself. He made the whole world beautiful and bright with just one hug. That is Christmas, and the land-people celebrate it every year," says Atlas, who has never spoken so much in all his life!
"Why don't they do it every day?" wonders Apollo the Goby.
"Even I don't know that, no one knows," answers Atlas, as he silently slips back into his dark cave.

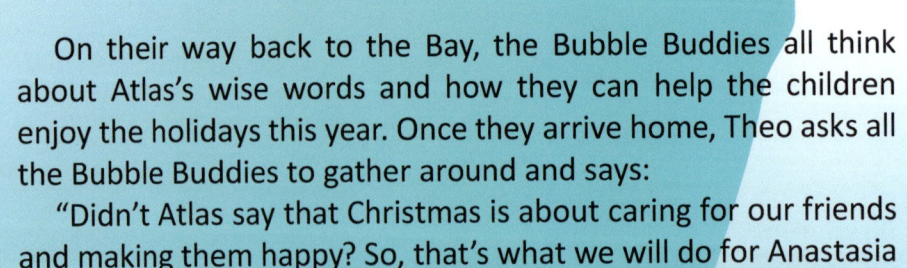

On their way back to the Bay, the Bubble Buddies all think about Atlas's wise words and how they can help the children enjoy the holidays this year. Once they arrive home, Theo asks all the Bubble Buddies to gather around and says:

"Didn't Atlas say that Christmas is about caring for our friends and making them happy? So, that's what we will do for Anastasia and Yanni! Since Christmas has been banned on land, we will celebrate it here, on the seabed. We will decorate Bubble Buddies Bay and fill the place with gifts for the children."

Theo turns to Athena, "Athena, can you organise a choir?"

"Yes, of course, and we'll sing their favourite Christmas songs that they call carols."

"I'll make some Christmas treats and little gifts for the children," adds Dimitra.

"Mmm, does Christmas treats mean food?" says Apollo dreamily.

"And I'll go and ask the electric eels and the glowing jellyfish," joins in Vassili and swims away.

"I'll do all the snipping," says Carci, snapping her raised claw.

King Adonis is all excited and swims around and around in little circles. "We will offer them the most beautiful Christmas they ever had."

Within a few hours, all the rocks are decorated with multicoloured sea anemones, while the ancient ruins are covered with golden plankton. Sea Stars decorate all the coral and caves, while the Electric Eels and the glowing Jellyfish light up the entire seabed. The Bubble Buddies' houses are filled with sea holly and covered with garlands of molluscs. In short, Bubble Buddies Bay is unrecognisable and more festive than ever.

They all smile and laugh with Vassili, who is dressed up as Father Christmas, while Carci, surrounded by many gifts, snips the ends of ribbons with her claws, making presents for all the island's children. Suddenly, King Adonis asks a question which, for a moment, wipes the smiles from their faces:

"And now, who is going to fetch the children?"

He is right. They have prepared it all beautifully, but how will they get the children here to see it?

Back at *The Steamed Oyster* Taverna, Anastasia and Yanni are looking through the glass into the empty aquarium. Behind them, Pierre carries a huge uncooked turkey on a tray heading towards the kitchen.

"Yanni!" exclaims Anastasia suddenly. "**What have we done?** Grab your mask and flippers. We're going for a dive!"

Yanni looks puzzled. He cannot understand what's got into Anastasia.

"King Adonis is a very rare tropical fish from China," continues Anastasia. "He will not be able to look after himself! We have to go and find him and bring him home!"

The two children run like the wind to the beach.

Below the water, the Bubble Buddies are gathered together.

"We need somebody who can go on land," says Theo.

"I can go on land," volunteers Carci.

"It's too dangerous," argues Dimitra.

"I'll fly over the Bay and check the coast is clear," suggests Athena.

"Perfect," concludes Theo, when there is a loud splash above their heads.

King Adonis swims around in little circles.

**"It's Anastasia and Yanni!"**

Anastasia and Yanni cannot believe their eyes when they see the seabed decorated for Christmas.

King Adonis whispers something into Carci's ear.
Anastasia and Yanni float before the Bubble Buddies. Anastasia makes a sign with her hands for a tropical fish, when Carci scurries towards her holding a gift-wrapped box in her claws above her head.
Anastasia takes the box, pulls on a ribbon, and out swims King Adonis!
"Surprise!"
It is a very special moment. King Adonis is happy to be going home. He has made lots of new friends and now knows the magic of Christmas.

Anastasia and Yanni swim away with King Adonis, and Yanni holds another gift to open back at the Taverna.

Mr Costas looks through the glass of the aquarium with a big smile, watching King Adonis, who is wearing a Christmas hat.

Anastasia and Yanni are sitting at a table with the second gift box. "Go on, open it," Anastasia tells Yanni. Yanni eagerly opens the box and out tumbles a huge, shimmering conch shell.

"Whoa!" Yanni smiles as he reaches for it. From seemingly far away, he hears gentle waves and the breeze across the sea. Yanni presses it to his ear and suddenly hears all the wonderful sounds of Bubble Buddies Bay inside. He excitedly hands it to Anastasia to try out.

"Now we will be able to listen to our new friends whenever we want!" says Anastasia with delight.

Just then, Mr Costas arrives and hands Anastasia a gift box.
"Merry Christmas, Anastasia," Mr Costas smiles.
Anastasia opens the box and pulls out a snow globe with an underwater sea theme.
"Ah, Daddy! I know this place."
"Shake it," Mr Costas says, all excited.

Snow falls and fish swim inside the dome. Anastasia stands and gives her father a big hug. Mr Costas whispers in her ear, "We will always have Christmas."

While Anastasia hugs Mr Costas, she sees the back of King Adonis wagging his tail looking out over Bubble Buddies Bay.

Athena, wearing a Christmas hat, flies up out of the sea and over the bay, waving her fin. Below her on the beach are many children going in and out of the sea: a Christmas miracle on a cold winter's day.
From far below, Anastasia and Yanni wave back at Athena.

Pierre rushes into the taverna. "Mr Costas, Mr Costas!" says Pierre, all in a panic, "There are hundreds of people coming this way."
"Customers, Pierre, customers. Bring out the turkey!"

MERRY FISHMAS TO EVERYBODY!

# Meet the Bubble Buddies

## KING ADONIS

Infamous resident of *The Steamed Oyster*, King Adonis is the most beautiful, colourful and dazzling Mandarinfish you'll ever see!

## VASILLI

A fun-loving, friendly Clownfish, Vasilli is always ready for an adventure or to help a buddy in need.

Clownfish live in anemones which protect them from predators, and the clownfish's bright colours lure fish in for the anemone to eat.

## ATHENA

The singing star of Bubble Buddies Bay, Athena is a talented Flying Fish who will wow you with a tune and her endless sparkle.

Flying fish can't really fly, but they can propel themselves out of the water to nearly 6m high!

## CARCI

Carci the Crab has lots of special skills including being able to cut with her sharp claws, and scuttle up onto land.

Mediterranean green crabs are omnivores - they eat both algae and small animals like mussels.

## APOLLO

Red-mouthed Gobies grow up to 18cm long

Adventure, food and more food are Apollo's favourite things. Always ready for some fun, Apollo is a Red-mouthed Goby who will play all day long! Until dinner time that is.

## DIMITRA

Dimitra the Octopus is caring, kind and a great cook! She loves to look after the other Bubble Buddies. Plus, if you need something done - just ask Dimitra!

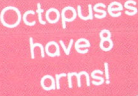

Octopuses have 8 arms!

## THEO

The Purple Sea Urchin is spiny but not dangerous. It can be held with care!

As a Sea Urchin, Theo is smaller than his friends, but he has a big personality. He's always ready for adventure and is just as brave as the larger Bubble Buddies.

## ATLAS

The oldest, wisest fish in Bubble Buddies Bay, visit Atlas the Anglerfish in his mysterious cave if you're looking for advice.

The deep sea is always very dark, as light from the sun doesn't reach down there. Some species of anglerfish produce their own source of light.

### Discover all the Buddies!

# Under the sea is the place to protect!

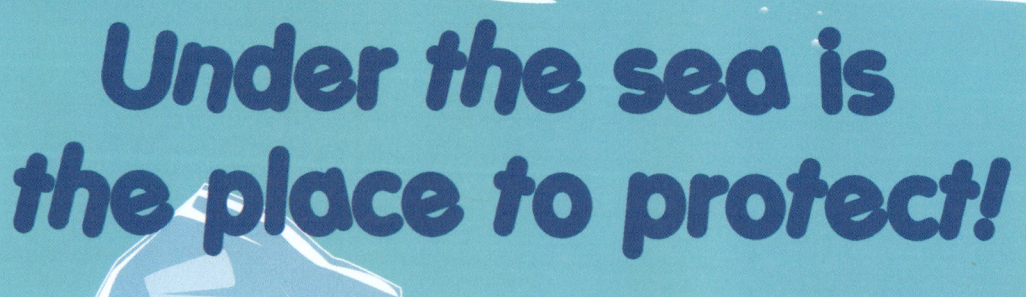

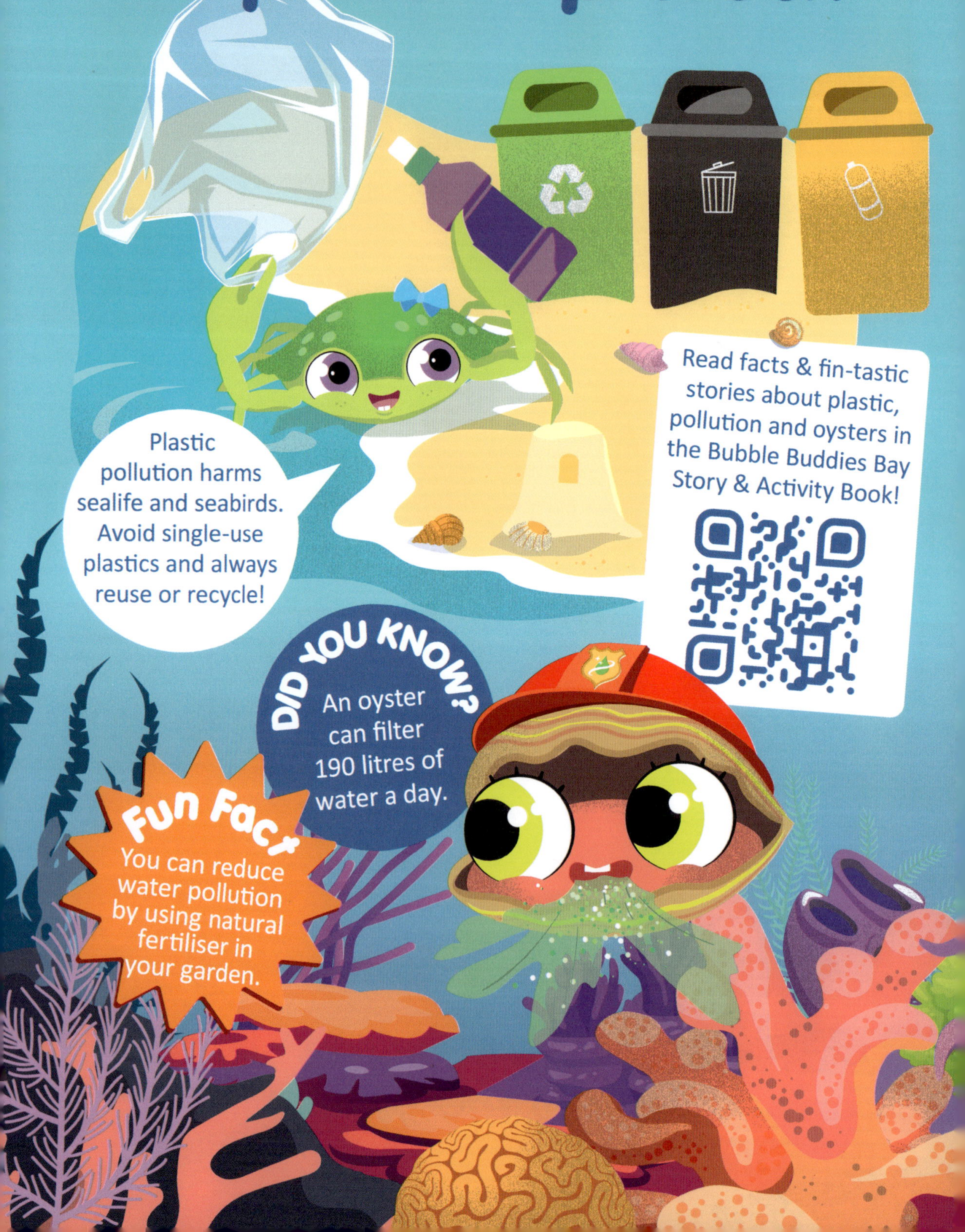

# Who is hiding here?

Unscramble the words and write them in the circles, then use the letters from the yellow circles to find the hidden word. Apollo has done the first one for you.

clues

ckro → r **o** c k

cta → ◯ ◯ ◯

stra → ◯ ◯ ◯ ◯

obx → ◯ ◯ ◯

sifh → ◯ ◯ ◯ ◯

o ◯ ◯ ◯ ◯ p u ◯

## Outstanding!

### Fact File

**Octopus**

*Scientific name:*
Octopoda

*Top speed:*
40km/h

*Body length:*
30cm - 5.4m

*Diet:*
Carnivore (meat)

**Clever camouflage**
Octopuses can change colour to blend in with their surroundings.

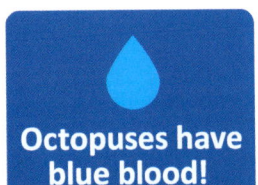

Octopuses have blue blood!

**What's for dinner?**
Adult octopuses eat crabs, snails, small fishes, and even other octopuses.

**Wearing a hat**
The Coconut Octopus carries a coconut shell on its head for protection!

# Meet the author

**George Lebesis** is a popular Greek children's author and music producer from Athens. In 2008, he created Greece's first children's festival, Town for Kids, and began writing books in 2010. His unpublished story *4 PAGES* won both the Original Story and Audience Awards at Fairy Tale Festival, and since then, Lebesis has become a beloved figure in Greek children's literature. His popular Fishsoup series, including *Merry Fishmas!*, has garnered widespread acclaim, becoming a staple in Greek school programs and a theatrical favourite. Fishsoup has been performed in theatres across Greece and Cyprus since 2010, including a musical adaptation staged at the Palace Theatre.

# Meet the illustrator

**Tamsin Baker** is a British illustrator currently living and working in rural Oxfordshire alongside her Greek rescue cat, Indie, who happens to look a lot like Anastasia's cat. Tamsin has two children who love visiting Greece and will proudly tell everyone they meet that their mummy draws the Bubble Buddies Bay fish.

Printed in Great Britain
by Amazon